The OFFICIAL
'7th Heaven
Scrapbook

Based on the hit TV series
created by Brenda Hampton

By Monica Rizzo

SCHOLASTIC INC.
New York   Toronto   London   Auckland   Sydney
Mexico City   New Delhi   Hong Kong

All photos courtesy of The WB

ISBN 0-439-16008-1

™ and © 2000 Spelling Television Inc.
All rights reserved. Published by Scholastic Inc.
SCHOLASTIC and associated logos are trademarks and/or registered trademarks of Scholastic Inc.

12 11 10 9 8 7 6 5 4 3 2 1   0 1 2 3 4 5 6/0
Printed in the U.S.A.
First Scholastic printing, March 2000

> ## "There's no greater feeling than the love of family . . . 7th Heaven"

Aaron Spelling is the famous Hollywood producer of many TV shows over the years including *The Love Boat, Melrose Place,* and *Beverly Hills, 90210. 7th Heaven* is one of his more recent shows, and in many ways, the one he's proudest of.

If his name is familiar to you, it's because he's the real-life dad of actors Tori [*90210*] and Randy [*Sunset Beach*] Spelling. And yes, he's very proud of them, too!

INTRODUCTION by Aaron Spelling

Hello, friends and welcome to the *7th Heaven Official Scrapbook.* I can hardly believe it was four years ago when the WB network came to me and said they wanted to do a show about a family. Time truly does fly when you're having fun.

I remember I was thrilled when I heard of the network's commitment to put a program on television that the whole family could watch and enjoy together. I knew it would be a challenge, since there weren't very many family-oriented shows on the air. Then I met with a woman by the name of Brenda Hampton, a producer who had an amazing concept about a functional family. That is, she had an idea that a husband and wife, and their five — no, make that seven — children could live under one roof harmoniously (with a few road bumps along the way, of course). And that's how the Camden family was created.

Over the years I've become more and more proud of the stories we tell each week on *7th Heaven.* We address some serious subject matter like racism, death, and gun control, but we also try to balance that with some comic relief from the likes of Simon and Ruthie. After all, you need a sense of humor in this world.

We strive to show you a real family, one where siblings argue and the kids don't listen to their parents. We know it's working because we've already been picked up for a fifth season! That means there will be a lot more Camden family adventures down the pike!

Because of you loyal fans, we're the number one show on the WB network. On behalf of Brenda, the cast and crew, and everybody at Spelling Television, thanks for making our family part of your family.

Aaron Spelling

BEGINNINGS

As Mr. Spelling noted, *7th Heaven* has its roots in a collaboration between himself, the WB network, and producer Brenda Hampton. That trio made for a winning combination — but the show didn't just "appear" on Monday nights after that. It took several months for writers to come up with the first script, and several more months to find the right actors to portray the Camden clan. Of course everything came together beautifully by the time the show aired its first episode in August 1996.

From the get-go, TV critics "got it" and gave *7th Heaven* a rousing two thumbs up! And so did television audiences. It didn't take long for fans to take the Camden family into their hearts, and into their homes.

FAMILY MATTERS

The Camdens, who live in the fictional California suburb of Glenoak, deal with the same issues all families deal with: whose turn it is to do the dishes, who's hogging the bathroom, and who needs help with homework. Each of the Camdens is an individual trying to make a place for him- or herself in the world. In a big family, that's not an easy task. And it just got bigger last season with the addition of two more Camdens, twins David and Samuel.

Over the years the Camden kids have learned and grown from the same types of experiences we have.

Oldest brother **MATT** fell in love with Heather (Andrea Ferrell), only to see her fall for another man. Now he's in college, has his own apartment and a job, and is in love with Shawna (Maureen Flannigan).

MARY has gone from responsible older sister/star of the Wildcat basketball team to a high school senior in search of her own identity. She doesn't always make the best choices (remember when she trashed the school gym?), and must live with the harsh consequences (losing her basketball scholarship).

SIMON is learning that puberty has its ups (steady girlfriend Deena) and downs (learning to shave for the first time). And **RUTHIE** is following in the footsteps of her older sister, Mary, by playing sports like soccer and football.

This season, middle sister **LUCY** has become concerned about her community and global issues. She now volunteers to help the homeless and women's rights organizations. But she hasn't always had this strength. When Lucy tried out for cheerleading, she initially lacked the self-confidence needed to succeed. She often compared herself to her older, more athletically inclined sister Mary. Thanks to her older brother Matt's words of encouragement, Lucy was able to find the inner strength she needed to make the squad.

TO THE TOP

This kind of inner support system is the backbone of the Camden clan. Admittedly, it sometimes seems too good to be true that a family would act this way. Actor Barry Watson, who plays Matt Camden, says, "We have a fantasy family that works. It's corny, but it's good corny. That's why people love it."

Indeed, *7th Heaven*'s fan base has increased so much that last year it became the WB's most-watched show! Ratingswise, it beats both *Dawson's Creek* and *Buffy the Vampire Slayer*.

In the pages of this book, you'll meet the magnificent seven and many others who make it all happen.

STAX OF FACTS

✮ *7th Heaven* premiered on August 26, 1996.

✮ The WB, like most networks, initially only committed to 13 episodes. But once they saw how quickly the show caught on with critics, they decided to renew it for the full season (22 episodes).

✮ Once a week wasn't enough. To satisfy the cravings of die-hard fans, the network began airing reruns of the show on Sunday nights, called *7th Heaven: Beginnings*.

✮ By its third season, *7th Heaven* had become the number one program with teens 12–17.

✮ Oh, baby! Because infants and toddlers are only allowed to work a certain number of hours each day, most TV shows hire twins to alternate in the role of one baby. But because *7th Heaven* has twice the need, producers found twice the solution by hiring *quadruplets*! The four babies who play Camden twins David and Samuel are Lorenzo, Zachary, Myrinda, and Nikolas Brino. Yep, one of 'em is a girl!

Camaro. In a house with seven children, Matt is the perfect "second father" to all of his brothers and sisters.

But sometimes Matt tries so hard to shield his siblings from adversity, he ends up suffering the most. When Mary took a dare from her friends and stole a glass from the Varsity, a high school hangout, Matt covered for her. Their dad, Eric, found the glass in the kitchen one morning and assumed Matt must have taken it. And instead of clarifying the situation, Matt decided he would take the punishment and protect Mary from Dad's wrath. In the end, Mary came clean. But she

CHAPTER ONE

BARRY WATSON
"Matt Camden"

Everyone should be so lucky to have a brother like Matt Camden. He's always quick to lend a hand, listen to your problems, or give you a ride to school in his cool black

appreciated what her older brother tried to do for her.

Matt is kind to all of his siblings. He often checks out the types of guys Mary and Lucy date, he regularly gives Simon advice about growing up, and in general steers Ruthie in the right direction. Plus he's always quick to lend a hand when their mom, Annie, needs help with the twins.

Matt's kindness and compassion extends beyond the Camden family, too. In fact, one of actor Barry Watson's favorite episodes was titled "Do Something," from the show's second season. "I took care of this boy who was sick and in the hospital," Barry explains. "Matt was supposed to be his guardian and spend time with him when his parents couldn't be there. It was probably one of the best relationships Matt has ever had with another character."

In another episode, from the show's third season, Matt walked away from peer pressure — drinking games in order to join a fraternity at Crawford College. But when a friend *couldn't* walk away and needed help, Matt was there to take care of him.

Because he's such a caring, loving person, it's no wonder Matt is such a hopeless romantic. He trekked all the way across the country just to talk to his ex-girlfriend Heather (Andrea Ferrell) after he learned that she had someone new in her life.

Not quite so romantic are Barry's real-life memories of that scene. "I traveled all that way to be with her and it was supposed to be cold as heck outside. So I was wearing layers of clothing, but in reality it was, like, one hundred degrees in the valley where we were shooting. If you actually watch it up close you can tell I'm sweating. I had so many layers on, they ended up having to cut the inside of my clothes out!"

IN REAL LIFE

Is Barry anything at all like Matt? You bet. "Hopefully the caring and nurturing part of Matt is a lot like me because I'm the same way with my family," Barry says, noting that he's the oldest of four kids. "I love my family so much," he adds.

Barry grew up in Traverse City, Michigan, and Dallas, Texas, before coming to Los Angeles to be an actor. He began modeling and acting when he was a teenager in Texas. A talent agent suggested he go to Los Angeles if he wanted to seriously pursue a career. Upon arriving in California, Barry did a series of commercials and guested on TV shows like *Baywatch*, *The Nanny*, and *Sister, Sister* before getting his big break — he played Seth in the short-lived 1996 television series *Malibu Shores*, which also starred fellow WB star Keri Russell (*Felicity*) and which was produced by Aaron Spelling. When Mr. Spelling was looking for an actor to play Matt Camden, he tapped Barry because of the good work he did on *Malibu Shores*.

EXTRA CURRICULAR ACTIVITIES

Last summer, Barry co-starred in the feature film *Teaching Mrs. Tingle* with *Dawson's Creek* star Katie Holmes (Joey) and acclaimed actress Helen Mirren. Although the film did not do well at the box office, it was an experience Barry relished. "I got to kiss Katie Holmes," he says with a grin.

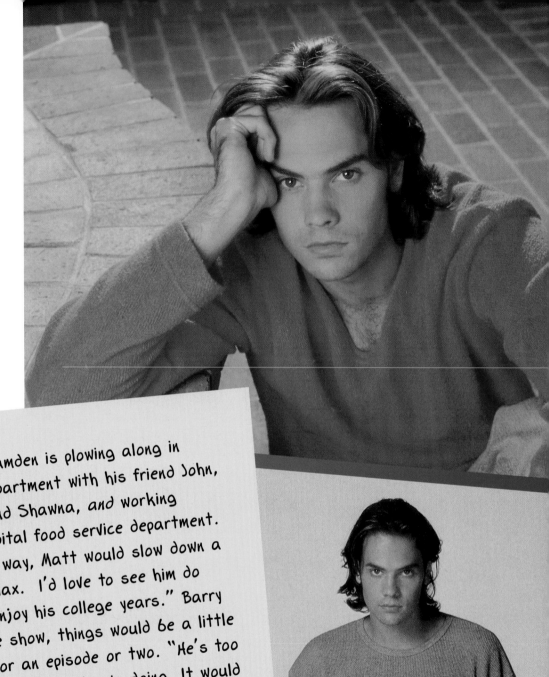

Although he would like to act in other films, Barry's first priority is *7th Heaven.* "I love working on this show. Everybody here is so cool. We all get along real great and it shows in our work."

PLOTLINES

Nowadays Matt Camden is plowing along in college, sharing an apartment with his friend John, happily dating girlfriend Shawna, and working part-time in the hospital food service department. But if Barry had his way, Matt would slow down a bit. "He needs to relax. I'd love to see him do something fun and enjoy his college years." Barry says if he wrote the show, things would be a little different for Matt for an episode or two. "He's too caught up in what everybody else is doing. It would be nice to see him have a fun evening out with his girlfriend."

BARRY WATSON
DID YOU KNOW?

BIRTH DATE: April 23, 1974
HOMETOWN: Born in Traverse City, Michigan, raised in Dallas, Texas
HEIGHT: 6'0"
WEIGHT: 170 lbs.
NAME GAME: Barry's real name is Michael Barret Watson
FAMILY AFFAIR: Two brothers, Scott and Kip, and one sister, Christie
A MATTER OF FACT: Barry collects memorabilia from the 1970s hit police show *Starsky and Hutch*, which was *also* produced by Aaron Spelling!
INTERESTS: He loves to hike in the hills

and canyons around his Los Angeles home with his four-and-a-half-year-old dog Harsky, a pit bull–golden retriever mix (whose name is a play on Barry's favorite old TV show). Barry cautions, "He's very territorial. Don't come over to my house and expect to come in. Once he knows you're okay, he's the sweetest dog in the world. Other than that, he'll probably jump through the window after you." (Note: His other dog, Stutch, now lives with a friend in Arizona.)
FAVORITE FOODS: Italian and Tex-Mex
FAVORITE ACTRESS: Patricia Arquette
FAVORITE MOVIES: *Valley Girl* and *Blue Velvet*
RANDOM QUOTE: "I don't watch TV much and I don't go to movies much. It's hard to be so involved with *7th Heaven* and then watch other shows. You start to critique everything because you're so involved."
PARALLEL LIVES: "My dad on *7th Heaven* deals with my character the same way my mom did with me when I was growing up," Barry once told *YM* magazine. "She taught me a lot of lessons that I didn't understand until I was older."

CHAPTER TWO

JESSICA BIEL
"Mary Camden"

Mary Camden is a typical all-American girl — pretty, but not frilly, athletic, and fashionable but not trendy. *7th Heaven's* creator Brenda Hampton once told *Entertainment Weekly* magazine she feels Mary is in some ways the most sensible kid in the family. And that certainly seems to be true.

Over the years, Mary has been in a variety of situations including dating Wilson (Andrew Keegan), a teenage single father, to unfairly prejudging a friend, to having major sibling rivalries with Matt and Lucy.

She's also shown a lot of determination about what she believes in, and the capacity for forgiveness. When Mary was injured in a hit-and-run accident, her leg was badly broken. But because basketball was such a big part of her life, she was determined to rehabilitate herself right back on the varsity squad. Mary even helped ease the driver's guilty conscience by forgiving him for what happened.

Mary does have a defiant streak, too. Remember the episode when she wanted a tattoo? Her parents, Eric and Annie, both said no, but she went ahead and got one on her ankle anyway — a Wildcat logo, which is the high school mascot.

BIEL FOR REAL

Of all of the Camden kids, actress Jessica "Jessie" Biel (rhymes with deal) is probably most like her character. The actress, who was named one of *People* magazine's 50 Most Beautiful People in 1999, is also very athletic in real life. While Mary is a star basketball player, Jessie excels in a variety of sports, including kickboxing, soccer, and surfing. "I grew up snowboarding in Colorado, but I've always thought surfing was really cool," she says. "I'm the kind of person who has to try things and even though I might fail, I'm going to practice and keep going until I get better."

It's that kind of determination that has helped her become a terrific actress. Jessie was born in Ely, Minnesota, but when she was in elementary school, her family moved to Boulder, Colorado. Because Jessie always enjoyed singing and dancing as a young girl, she soon began performing in local musical theater productions like *The Sound of Music* and *Beauty and the Beast*.

Jessie received a lot of encouragement from her family to pursue her dreams. She's proud of her ethnic heritage ("I'm German, French, English, and American Indian — and a lot of other things, too"), and she's proud of being her own woman. A self-described "chunk" when she was a young girl, Jessie refused (and still does) to obsess over counting calories. "I definitely have a good perspective," she told *People.* "I love food too much."

Jessie did some modeling in Colorado before traveling with her family to California for a talent competition in 1994 — she came in first. That's when she and the family moved to Los Angeles where she continued modeling for fashion campaigns like the store Limited Too. In 1996, Jessie landed the Mary Camden role.

EXTRA CURRICULAR

Although she's extra-busy balancing *7th Heaven* and high school, Jessie still takes the opportunity to act in movies. Jessie played Peter Fonda's granddaughter in the critically acclaimed movie *Ulee's Gold*, and in 1998 she and Jonathan Taylor Thomas co-starred in *I'll Be Home for Christmas*. Multi-tasking and working hard is another place where she and Mary connect. "We're just so much alike it's kind of hard to think of something that's different!" Jessie admitted.

Jessie loves the variety of stories *7th Heaven* tells. "You get to do a lot of different things on this show," she told *Entertainment Weekly*. "Some of the story lines are heavy, like Mary taking a power-booster drug for her basketball team, and some of them are light, so you have to be able to do comedy, too."

These days *7th Heaven* has Jessie's full commitment. Well, that and school. Now a senior in high school, Jessie, along with her TV siblings David Gallagher and Mackenzie Rosman, puts in a minimum of three hours of on-set tutoring each day.

Just like Mary, Jessie hits the books hard and wants to go to college someday. Jessie, who loves traveling, the outdoors, and photography, is keeping her options open. "I have one more year of high school, which seems like it's going to take forever — and then I'm on my own."

JESSICA BIEL
DID YOU KNOW?

BIRTH DATE: March 3, 1982

HOMETOWN: Born in Ely, Minnesota, raised in Danbury and Simsbury, Connecticut, and Boulder, Colorado

HEIGHT: 5' 7 1/2"

PERSONALLY SPEAKING: Jessica's dad, Jon, is a business consultant, and her mom, Kim, is a homemaker. She also has a younger brother, Justin.

FAVORITE FOODS: Mashed potatoes, steamed broccoli, and Mexican. "I love fajitas!" Jessie enthuses.

FAVORITE ACTRESSES: Jodie Foster, Winona Ryder, and Susan Sarandon

FAVORITE ACTOR: Sean Connery

DOUBLE TROUBLE: Her best friend is a girl whose name is also Jessie! The two pals have known each other since the fifth grade. The friend, who lives in Colorado, says geography and fame hasn't changed friendship with her actress pal one bit. "Jessica is still the same goofy, down-to-earth girl she was when she left," Jessie told *Jump* magazine.

ADVENTURESOME JESSIE: She recently traveled in Europe with two of her friends — her first non-family vacation ever.

FRIEND TO THE END: Her secret to lasting friendship? Never stay mad. "If I was in a fight with a friend, I would just call and be like, what is the deal? What did I do? What do we need to talk about? How can we get it over with?"

FACE VALUE: Jessica hates wearing makeup! She told *People* magazine, "I have to wear so much on the show that the last thing I want to do when I come home is suffocate my face."

RANDOM QUOTE: Jessie's advice to wannabe performers? "Take acting classes and have fun. If you don't have fun, you are in the wrong business because there is so much work you have to do with all this and if it's not fun, you are in the wrong business."

CHAPTER THREE

BEVERLEY MITCHELL
"Lucy Camden"

Lucy Camden is the kind of girl you want to have as a best friend. She's loyal, caring, and loves going to the mall. But because Lucy is a middle child, and a year younger than her pretty, popular, athletic older sister, Mary, she's often struggled with finding her own identity.

Always eager to fit in, Lucy has gone against her own better judgment from time to time. When some girls came over for a sleepover, they convinced Lucy to hide under the bed. While she did, her "friends" encouraged others in the group to talk about her and say bad things including what they didn't like about her. Some friends.

Like most people, Lucy wants to be accepted and loved. She's getting there. Now a junior in high school, Lucy has evolved over the years from a boy crazy teenager into a young woman. She no longer spends all of her free time on the phone keeping up with her peers. Instead, she's focusing on her studies and spending her free time helping others. In season four, against the advice of some of the "popular" kids in high school, Lucy reached out and began volunteering for Habitat for Humanity, a non-profit organization that helps build housing for low-income and homeless families.

A GIRL WITH A HEART

It's precisely this humanitarianism that makes Beverley Mitchell so special. This veteran actress is always quick to participate in a fundraiser or help others in her community. Recently she spent an afternoon at a Pacoima, California, elementary school and helped paint murals, plant flowers, and, of course, sign tons of autographs for her adoring fans!

At age four, Beverley got her start in acting quite accidentally — she threw a tantrum in a Los Angeles area store when she wasn't allowed to get a toy she wanted! A talent manager happened to be there and was so impressed with Beverley's spunk, he gave her mom his business card. Soon after, the tyke began acting in commercials for AT&T, Oscar Mayer, and Cream of Wheat. TV roles followed on shows like *Quantum Leap*, *Baywatch*, *Melrose Place*, *Big Brother Jake*, and TV movies.

In 1996, Beverley was called in to try out for *7th Heaven*. But the audition didn't go very well and Beverley was disappointed because she really wanted the part. Luckily her manager was able to arrange another meeting, and this second chance was all Beverley needed to prove she was the right person to play Lucy Camden.

REAL-LIFE LESSONS

It's no wonder *7th Heaven* is close to Beverley's heart. What makes it even more special is the terrific fan response she receives, which makes her feel like she's really making a difference in people's lives.

There are many episodes that have touched her deeply. For example, in the show's third season, Lucy discovers one of her friends is a "cutter" — someone who repeatedly mutilates his or her own body with sharp objects. "I didn't even know people did that," Beverley admitted. "Then I found out one of my own friends in real life had been a scratcher, which is very similar to the situation in the show. She would scratch herself until she would bleed. I'd find welts on her hands and she'd say 'Oh, my cat scratched me.' You don't know people can be in such pain. I got a letter from a girl who was a cutter and she said she never knew there were other people out there like that. After she saw our show, she went to get help. I'm in awe of the power our show has over people. I'm honored that I can be a part of something like this, where people have these problems and are able to find answers in our show."

It's not only Beverley's fans who find answers to life's issues from the show. So does she. "There are a lot of situations in the show that make me think back to my

from people. One girl wrote to me and said she lost her best friend and her best friend's sister in an accident and she thought it was her fault. She was thinking about committing suicide until she watched our show and realized that life goes on and she wasn't to blame. To affect someone in that way — to give a person the strength to stay alive is amazing. That's a positive message our show sends."

own life and realize I might have been wrong, or I should have thought about things."

One of season three's most powerful episodes centered around a friend of Lucy's dying in a car accident. Sadly, that one was especially close to Beverley — because in real life one of her best friends was killed in an accident. When Producer Brenda Hampton learned of the tragedy, she asked Beverley how she'd feel if the show did an episode on that topic. Initially Beverley was reluctant because the subject matter hit so close to home. But after talking it over with her mother, her friends, and Brenda, she agreed it was an important show to do.

Beverley reasoned, "The situations were completely different, but the pain was real. It brought up all of these real emotions that I basically never dealt with when I was grieving a couple years ago. I still get fan letters

MAKING THE GRADE

While Lucy is still in high school, Beverley is now a college freshman majoring in film. How does she balance school and work? Very carefully! "Tuesdays and Thursdays I have two classes, from eight a.m. — ten-forty a.m. As soon as I'm done, I come to work. I do my homework in between scenes. It's intense, but it's worth it. I want to be in show business for the rest of my life, but I also know I need a good education."

While Beverley, an only child in real life, enjoys living in the dorms at her Los Angeles university, she's most at home on the 7th Heaven set. "I feel like this is my home away from home! I've adopted six brothers and sisters and two new parents. Plus, the whole crew is like a family to me, too. We all look out for each other. If I ever needed any of them, they would jump to help me. And I would do the same for them. We're really lucky."

BEVERLEY MITCHELL
DID YOU KNOW?

BIRTH DATE: January 22, 1981

HOMETOWN: Pasadena, California

HEIGHT: 5' 2"

A MATTER OF FACT: Lucy Camden is a year *younger* than Mary. But in real life, Beverley is actually a year *older* than Jessica Biel (Beverley is a freshman in college and Jessica is a high school senior.)

NAME GAME: No ordinary girl, *this* Beverley spells her name with an extra "e." And yes, it's misspelled by others *much*.

FAMILY: Mom, Sharon, is an office manager. Dad, David, is an independent car race organizer.

FAVORITE FOODS: Steak, lobster, and clam chowder. "If I go to a restaurant on fridays and they don't have my soup I get upset!"

CAT FANCY: Beverley has two cats, Tigger and Casper.

FRAIDY CAT: You won't see Beverley renting the *Scream* series anytime soon. "I'm not one to watch scary movies. I saw *Seven* and I about died. I had a stuffed gorilla and I had that thing in my mouth so I would not scream! I was so scared!"

FAVORITE ACTRESS: Jodie Foster

FAVORITE ACTOR: Bill Paxton

FAVORITE BOOK: *Black Beauty*

TUNING IN: "Anything that's on the radio I will listen to."

AT HOME: While Beverley doesn't have any siblings in real life, she wonders what it would be like if she were in Lucy's shoes. "I cannot picture all those kids and one bathroom. That would be too complicated!"

RANDOM QUOTE: "My dad used to call me Monkey. I used to climb into everything."

CHAPTER FOUR

DAVID GALLAGHER
"Simon Camden"

Simon is arguably the glue of the Camden family. When there's a crisis, Simon can usually be found in the middle trying to resolve it. When big brother Matt needed money, young Simon gladly lent a hand. Simon was also there for Ruthie when she was afraid to swim. He helped her get over her fear of the water by teaching her the basics in the family bathtub.

And while he's very supportive of his six brothers and sisters, Simon constantly strives for what *he* wants, too. In the show's very first episode, he pushed and pleaded with his parents to allow him to get a dog (Happy, of course). They gave in when they saw how Simon and Happy made a perfect pair. The pooch provides *7th Heaven* with a dose of comic relief, like the time Simon and Ruthie ordered red rain boots from the "Eddie Bowser" catalog for her.

When the baby twins arrived, Simon rose to the occasion and took it upon himself to help out with chores and keep Ruthie focused on her homework. Helpful older bro and go-getter: That's pretty much who David Gallagher is, too. With one exception. "I don't think I'm quite as nice to my real-life brothers and sisters as Simon is," David says with a grin.

DAVID'S REAL DEAL

While Simon is the sibling smack in the middle of the Camden household, David is the eldest of five kids in real life. "I'm usually the 'Matt' in my family. I'm looking out for the younger ones, making sure they don't do anything wrong. And sometimes I push my weight around a little bit when I can. I say, you know, 'Hey, I did this for you, [now] clean my room.'"

ROLL THE CREDITS

David is a veteran actor whose credits include the films *Look Who's Talking Now*, *Phenomenon*, and *Richie Rich's Christmas Wish*. He got his start in his hometown of Queens, New York. His mom answered an ad in the local paper for an open call audition and David, only a year old, got the job as a baby model. More modeling and commercials followed until David started landing TV movie and feature film roles. When he was 11, David had more acting experience than some grown-up actors. No wonder he landed the role of Simon over hundreds of other actors when he read for *7th Heaven*'s producers.

LIFE LESSONS

Now a freshman in high school, David says being on the show has taught him a lot about what's important in life, like tolerance and acceptance of others. "The episode that really hit home for me was the Holocaust episode where Simon learns about Auschwitz and what Hitler did to the Jewish people. Simon realizes this *wasn't* a hoax, that it really *did* happen, especially after he talks to a real Holocaust survivor."

David admits that like a lot of kids his age, he didn't know much about the subject. "It was never something that captured my attention until we did this show. It was a piece of history I never really knew. So when we did the episode, I studied about it and read everything I could. It's still hard to

accept that this really happened. But it did."

David feels that particular episode encapsulates what *7th Heaven* is all about. "It was a challenge every one of us accepted with open arms because those kinds of episodes make *7th Heaven* what it is."

That's why David says he'll never attempt to write an episode of *7th Heaven* any time soon. "Besides, they'd never let me do that because if I did, the show would not be an hour long, it would be four hours long!"

Indeed, David envisions a Simon-a-thon that would indulge every one of his fantasies! A real-life car fanatic, David says if he had his way, "Simon would win the lottery and get twenty Prowlers [expensive precision automobiles] of different colors — it's my dream vehicle. He'd also have one or two Vipers [also cars]. Simon would become an

aggressive blader, plus he would save the rainforest, help people and do good things. And he'd be popular, too."

Not that Simon isn't already popular. "He's popular in a quirky sort of way." In fact, this year Simon got a hip new spiky haircut and a steady girlfriend. But not much else has changed, David maintains. "People appreciate Simon and the way he is."

David's future plans are to continue working in film and television after graduating from college. Even though he's only a freshman, David is tackling college prep courses like honors literature and honors geometry. "I will keep acting until I get out of high school. Then I'll go to college and study film or cinematography or directing. But I won't act when I'm in college — nothing will interfere with my studies."

DAVID GALLAGHER
DID YOU KNOW?

BIRTH DATE: February 9, 1985

HOMETOWN: Queens, NY

HEIGHT: 5' 6" and growing!

PERSONALLY SPEAKING: David has a real-life *7th Heaven* going on at home with Mom, Elena, Dad, Vince, and his two brothers — Kyle and Killian, and two sisters — Michelle and Kelly

PETS: Two turtles, five birds, and two Rottweiler dogs named Nomad and Sonia

FAVORITE MEAL: Steak, mashed potatoes with gravy, corn on the cob, stuffing, and buttered noodles

FAVORITE ACTRESSES: Rene Russo and Vanessa L. Williams

FAVORITE ACTOR: John Travolta. Lucky David has worked with his idol on two feature films — *Phenomenon* and *Look Who's Talking Now.*

STICKS AND STONES: The cast and crew like to tease David about his new haircut. His nickname on the set is "Spike."

RANDOM QUOTE: "There's a little bit of me in Simon, like my facial expressions, the way I look, the way I move my eyebrows. Since I cut my hair, everyone is telling me they can see how much my face really moves when I'm talking."

CHAPTER FIVE

MACKENZIE ROSMAN
"Ruthie Camden"

With a nickname like Mack, you know little Mackenzie Rosman must be cool! Known on the set for her sweet disposition and irresistible charm, Mack is very much like her character Ruthie. "We both love animals a lot," she says.

When she first started on *7th Heaven*, Mack was only five years old. But now the ten-year-old fifth-grader is ready to tackle some bigger scenes, like season four's first episode where Ruthie was supposed to keep a secret about her Aunt Julie getting married. She blabs it to Aunt Julie's father (Ruthie's grandfather, "The Colonel"), which upsets her parents and siblings. In the end, Ruthie's carelessness didn't harm anyone, but she began to understand the value of earning someone's trust.

Mack's favorite episodes are the ones where she delivers the laughs. "I liked when I got to work with the chimpanzee. Ruthie kept telling everyone she saw a monkey out in the tree, but nobody believed her. They thought it was Ruthie's imagination," Mack explains. In the end it turns out the monkey was real, a neighbor's pet to be exact, and everyone apologized for not believing Ruthie. But who could blame them? After all, Ruthie *did* have an imaginary friend named Hoowie.

QUICK LEARNER

Like her television siblings Beverley Mitchell and David Gallagher, Mack got an early start in show business. Soon after Mack was born in Charleston, South Carolina, her family moved to Los Angeles. When she was three, she did several commercials, including a national spot for Hormel hot dogs. Then, at age five, she auditioned for the role of little Ruthie. "I'm pretty lucky," Mack says. "It all happened so fast for me."

When she's not working on her homework or learning her lines, Mack plays with *7th Heaven*'s Happy or her own dog, a two-year-old Yorkie named Molly. "I bring her to work every day," Mack says of her four-legged pal. Molly is hoping to become a performing dog like Happy. She obeys Mack's commands to sit, beg, jump, and speak. But Molly's favorite thing to do is nap while resting in Mack's arms.

WORKING GIRL

Lately, Mack has had less time to play with Molly, thanks to her expanding presence on the show and blossoming movie career. Mack did a movie last summer called *Gideon's Web*, and she's auditioning for other big screen rolls. Despite *7th Heaven*'s popularity, and the new movie, Mack stresses that she's still "just a normal girl. When I'm not at work I go to my regular school. The kids there watch the show, but they don't treat me special. They know me because I'm me. I like that."

The same goes for Mack's younger brother, Chandler, who likes being who *he* is. "He tried acting once but he didn't like it. And that's okay. He has lots of activities he likes better, like soccer and karate."

WISHFUL THINKING

In real life, Mack has dogs, cats, and horses. So it's no wonder her dream episode would include lots of animals. "I'd get to ride my horse and have lots and lots of animals and live in a big house."

7th Heaven is the coolest job Mack could ever imagine. "Everyone here is really nice. I hang out sometimes with David and Beverley," she says with a grin. "But I like Happy the best."

MACKENZIE ROSMAN
DID YOU KNOW?

BIRTH DATE: December 28, 1989

HOMETOWN: Charleston, South Carolina

HEARTY APPETITE: One of the first jobs Mack sank her teeth into was a commercial for Hormel hot dogs. "It was cool because I got to eat hot dogs and cotton candy all day!"

CROWDED HOUSE: In addition to younger brother, Chandler, and mom, Donna, Mack has a Noah's ark assortment of pets: two thoroughbred horses, Easy Mocha and Xena Warrior Princess; two dogs, Molly and Gizmo; two birds, Fiddle and Diddle; two cats, Eddie and Chance; two goldfish ("I forget their names," Mack confesses).

CHORES: It's Mack's job to feed all of the family pets.

FAVORITE PASTIME: "I *love* to read," Mack says.

HOBBIES: Horseback riding, and playing with all of the family pets

RANDOM QUOTE: Mack was used to being the youngest on the show, until the Camden twins came along. "They're funny because when we are working, they make little noises during scenes. They drop stuff or throw it on the ground."

CHAPTER SIX

STEPHEN COLLINS
"Reverend Eric Camden"

Eric Camden is a loving husband, devoted father to seven children, and a dedicated minister to the parishioners of his Glenoak, California, church. And while he seems to have the answers to all of life's mysteries, viewers learned over the past three and a half seasons that he's very human.

Portrayed by actor Stephen Collins, Eric Camden deals with the same issues many dads deal with — kids wanting tattoos, dat-ing, drugs and alcohol, being a provider for the family. Eric practices what he preaches, leads by example, admits when he's wrong, and most of all, learns from his mistakes.

Eric also has a lighter side, as evidenced by all of those think-tank sessions at the neighborhood pool hall with Matt and Lucy! The same can be said of Stephen, who's married and has a nine-year-old daughter. The veteran actor was raised outside New York City and deftly mixes pleasure (he's active in his community and regularly partici-pates as a lay eucharistic minister at his Los Angeles Episcopalian church) and business (he's a twice-published novelist and an accomplished stage and film actor).

The beginning of the fourth season threw Eric for a huge loop — he suffered a heart attack. It was a message for him to slow down and enjoy life and all of its offer-ings. It taught him you can't be everything to all people. And what matters most to Eric is his family.

David Gallagher feels the same can be said about Stephen. "He's like a second father to me. He's really fun to hang out with and talk about sports, and he always encour-ages us to read and study. He really cares about us and that means a lot."

CATHERINE HICKS
"Annie Camden"

As if five kids weren't enough, Annie Camden gave birth to twins in *7th Heaven*'s third season, making her the busiest homemaker on television! It's a role actress Catherine Hicks cherishes — today, that is. But several years ago she admits she wasn't sure how America would embrace a stay-at-home mom.

"When I first got this job, I kept saying to Brenda [Hampton, *7th*'s creator], 'Couldn't Annie go to law school at night?' I was a little embarrassed that maybe women in the audience wouldn't respect me."

Then the reality of motherhood hit Catherine, who has a seven-year-old daughter of her own. "Being a mom in real life helps me play Annie. I couldn't do this role without having given birth and raised a baby, in terms of the nurturing, the hugging, understanding a little person."

And the show, in turn, helps Catherine with her real-life parenting dilemmas. "I think because I say these lines every day, it helps me because I'm not strict at home. We're strict parents on the show and it's not politically correct to be that way because it's sort of old-fashioned. But I think people are starting to come around and say it's okay to be that way." In fact, "It dawned on me as I looked around at my friends, that there are many Annie Camdens in the world, these supermoms. In fact, every mom I know in Los Angeles is that way."

A native of Scottsdale, Arizona, Catherine has adjusted wonderfully to helping helm the Camden household with her minister husband. And that's largely thanks to the support she's received from fans around the country. "Fans write in, moms love it. I think we actually help parents to parent. Gun control, teens dating — I know from the fan mail we get that we help with some specific problems. That's why people love our show. Because we're a family, we stick it out. We're in it for the long haul."

CHAPTER SEVEN

HAPPY
"Happy"

Ask anyone on the *7th Heaven* set who their favorite castmate is and most often the answer is Happy, the white terrier mix pooch Simon adopted in the show's very first episode.

Happy (her real name, too) kind of fell into acting after being adopted from a Los Angeles veterinarian's office as a puppy. Several years ago Happy visited the set of *Mad About You* (Happy and *Mad About You* dog star Murray were friends). That's where *7th Heaven*'s creator, Brenda Hampton, met

Happy and thought she'd be perfect for the Camdens. Needless to say, it was a match made in, well, heaven!

Happy's trainer, Shawna Suffredini of Boone's Animals for Hollywood, says Happy, who's now four years old, is ecstatic about her TV family. "She likes the whole cast, but especially David and Mackenzie because she spends the most time working with them."

When she's on the set, Happy has to go through hair and makeup just like all of the other actors. "We have to wash her and brush her long hair," Shawna explains. "It takes half a day!" And that's not all. "She gets her teeth cleaned a lot so she's ready for the camera. And we sometimes have to trim her bangs because the camera guys say they can't see her eyes."

Maintaining eye contact with her human co-stars, the show's director, and Shawna is important for Happy. "I always have to be where she can see me so she can see my commands," Shawna says.

So far, so good. Happy's best episodes have been those where she's teamed with Simon and Ruthie. "In the past she's had to wear different costumes little Ruthie would dress her up in — tutus and feather boas. A really funny one was when the kids ordered doggie rain boots out of a catalog and paid for them with a credit card that arrived in Happy's name. At the end of the show, Happy had to come downstairs wearing the boots. Another episode was when she had supposedly won a dog food contest and Simon had to teach her a trick, which was to roll over, play dead, and cover her eyes. She did a really great job with that one."

In between scenes, Happy plays with Mackenzie and the rest of the cast or grabs a nap in her air-conditioned dressing room. When she's at home, four-year-old Happy enjoys playing with the other animals at the Boone's ranch in Castaic, California. "When she's off we let her be a dog and do her own thing. But when we have to go to work, she's always ready to jump in the truck and go! She loves working!"

DID YOU KNOW?

BIRTH DATE: July 14, 1995

WEIGHT: 35 pounds

SOLO ACT: Many dog performers, like "Eddie" from *Frasier*, have lookalike doubles to help share the workload. But because Happy is so unique-looking, her trainer hasn't been able to find another dog to help out.

FAVORITE FOOD: Meaty snacks like chicken and sausage

HOBBIES: Running, playing with children

HERE, KITTY, KITTY: Happy loves cats! She plays with the Boone's Animals for Hollywood cats all the time.

FAVORITE TRICK: Covering her eyes with one of her paws

PERSONAL APPEARANCES: Happy's been on the E! network and recently attended the TV Guide Awards.

FAN MAIL: Happy hasn't mastered using a pen, so she has someone help her answer her mail. If you write to her, she promises she'll try to write back.

CHAPTER EIGHT

BEHIND THE SCENES

It all looks so real on TV, but in truth the Camden household is actually a movable set based in a Santa Monica, California, "warehouse," also known as a soundstage. The "real" two-story white Craftsman house actually belongs to a private citizen who gave *7th Heaven* permission to photograph and show its *exterior* each week. The kitchen is actually a three-walled room, as is the dining room, living room, and bedrooms. Where a "fourth" wall would normally be is where the *cameras* are instead.

The reason the show is shot on a soundstage is because a lot of people are involved in bringing the Camden family adventures to America's living rooms each week. A director, makeup artist, lighting designer, script supervisor, producers, camera operators, and the actors are just *some* of the many people who need to see what's going on at all times. In order to accommodate them, the rooms have to be "open," as if they are looking into a store window display.

DRESSING ROOMS

Outside of the large soundstage are several camper trailers parked side by side. Inside each trailer is a couch, a table and chairs, a television—VCR unit, a refrigerator, and a radio. These trailers serve as dressing rooms for the actors. This is where the cast reads scripts, makes phone calls, and rests in between scenes. Beverley often brings her laptop computer to work so she can catch up on college assignments and send e-mails. David and Jessica talk on the phone, do homework, and visit with each other, while Mackenzie likes to read and play with her dog, Molly. And when Barry is on a break, he enjoys sitting in a shaded spot outside of his trailer and drinking a fresh cup of coffee. After all — as *he* likes to tease David — *he* doesn't have homework any more.

SCHOOL DAYS

While Barry is able to kick it when he's not working on set, David, Jessica, and Mackenzie have to go to school. The classrooms are located in mini trailers on the other side of the big soundstage. David, Jessica, and Mackenzie are required to have three hours of schoolwork each day. Teachers from their regular schools supply an on-set tutor with lesson plans, so that the young actors can keep up with what kids in their grade are doing. To fulfill their science lab requirements, once or twice a month a teacher (his name is "Science Bob") brings his mobile lab to the set. He prepares biology and chemistry experiments for Jessica, David, and Mackenzie to do. Sometimes they examine live animals, like iguanas or hissing cockroaches, and other times they concoct potions in beakers.

FUN 'N' GAMES

While this group works awfully hard each week, they do have fun. It's not uncommon to see Barry, David, and Stephen discussing sports, or Beverley and Jessica talking about school and (what else?) boys. Everyone likes to tickle and tease Mackenzie, or hold one of the adorable Brino quadruplets. As Barry says, "We've all got such great relationships with

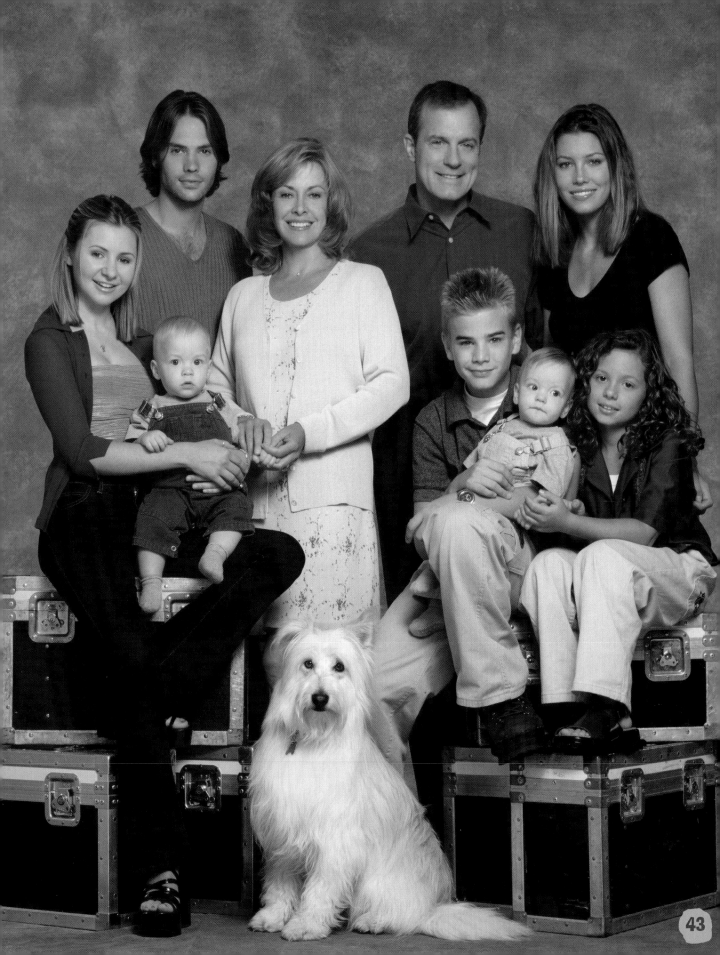

each other and from what I hear from the fans, they say they can really *tell* we all get along."

Sometimes the actors even like to make up their own scenes to act out. David explains, "Barry is actually known as Buck. He and Stephen have this skit called 'Bucky and the Rev.' Bucky and the Rev are Matt Camden and Eric Camden by day, but by night they fight crime. Each of us has a part. Beverley plays a nutso secretary, Jessie plays a girl who's always getting killed and comes back in the end, kind of like Kenny on *South Park*. And I'm their weapons supplier."

"We really like each other," Catherine enthuses. "Everyone here just happens to be very funny and we just crack each other up. There's no big egos here."

You probably won't see "Bucky and the Rev" on *7th Heaven* any time soon. But it is just one of the many ways this cast enjoys spending time together. Over the past three and a half seasons, they've grown to love one another like a family. Perhaps David says it best: "Everybody is so familial and nice to each other and we all treat each other with the same respect."

CHAPTER NINE

7TH HEAVEN CYBER STYLE

Can't get enough of your favorite *7th Heaven* stars? Want to learn more about the show? The Internet is a great place to explore. Just go to the show's official web sites. Here's what you'll find:

OFFICIAL 7TH HEAVEN WEB SITES

www.thewb.com

Show information, photos, video trailers of upcoming episodes, links to other WB shows like *Dawson's Creek*, *Felicity*, *Roswell*, and *Buffy the Vampire Slayer*.

www.virtuallot.com

General information about the show, cast bios, chat rooms, interactive games, and links to other Warner Bros. shows and movies.

FAN MAIL

All of the *7th Heaven* stars agree that they love hearing from the show's loyal fans. It makes them feel good — no, make that *great*, about the hard work they do each week. So if you've got something you'd like to share with any of the show's actors (that goes for Happy, too), go ahead and drop a line. They try to answer as much mail as possible. But sometimes it can get overwhelming because, after all, this is a popular group!

The address is: *7th Heaven* c/o The WB Television Network, 3701 Oak Street, Burbank, CA 91505

CHAPTER TEN

THAT'S A WRAP!

The third season of *7th Heaven* was by far one of the most exciting on television. We saw Matt go off to college, Lucy and Mary continue to struggle with high school dilemmas, and Simon become interested in girls. But most exciting of all was when Annie gave birth to twins David and Samuel.

In season four, we found out that Annie has a breaking point. She enlisted Eric, Mary, Lucy, and Simon to help out around the house. Matt managed to keep his head above water by juggling college, work, and his relationship with Shawna.

Meanwhile, as Lucy continued to come into her own as a young woman, *Mary* started to unravel. Her college basketball scholarship was jeopardized when she got mixed up with the wrong crowd. Simon continued his quest to figure out girls, and Ruthie continued to make us laugh.

And as Mr. Spelling notes in his introduction, a fifth season is already in the works. What lies ahead? Only Brenda Hampton knows at this point and she's not telling. Will Matt and Shawna get married? Will Mary go to college? What will the twins say when they start talking? As the expression goes — Keep it tuned!